A
DELMA DESIGN
COLLECTIONS
PUBLICATION

Jim Jim Bear.

Jim Jim's short for gymnast.
He is an active bear –
Likes to practise knee-bends
And knows a gymnasium where
The ropes are considerably thicker
And suitably Teddy Bear weight,
And where the instructors are hearty
And never overweight!
Jim Jim manages back-bends
And standing on one foot,
Swivels his ears independently
(His eyes have a glassy look).
Swings each arm around him
And touches his knee with his chin,
Wriggles his toes on the carpet
And swivels his head in a spin.
Participates in wrestling
And armlocks with Dreaded Sam,
Plays tennis with Monica Fullbody
And rounders with Slippery Dan.
And when the gymnasium's deserted
He knows it's time for tea –

Cycles to Auntie Gertie's
As fit as a bear can be!

Nigel Bear.

When Nigel heard of Wombles
And the wastes of Wimbledon,
He rolled his eyes within his head
And murmured, "Oh what fun!"
For Wimbledon means strawberries
  And lots of Jersey cream,
  And bouncing balls
  And tennis nets
  And courts all emerald green,
  And umpires calling "In" and "Out"
  And "Love" and "Deuce" and "Game"!
  And champion bears from the world of sport –
  (And once a princess played!)

Now when my Uncle Ponsonby
Took luncheon with the Queen,
They had to leave their trifle
To see the opening game –
For Rollo Bear was playing,
(He's the champion bear by far),
And after bowing to the box
Lopped the ball beyond her car,
Swotted at a bumble-bee
And waved his racket high,
Returned the serves adroitly

Turning cartwheels in the sky.
And when the game was over
And Rollo Bear had won,
The Queen beckoned Ponsonby over
And bade him "With her come –
To present the cup to the winner" –
The Wimbledon Grand Trophy,
And afterwards invited Rollo
To join her for Buckingham tea.

Bertie Bear.

Bertie Bear is practising.
He hopes to be a clown –
Throws his wig into the air
And bounces up and down.
Juggles with a flower pot
And half a dozen eggs,
Blows a squeaky whistle
And walks on rubbery legs.
Tickles with a hairy mop
And trips into a clown,
Adjusts his yellow, spotty spats
And slithers to the ground.

Bertie Bear is practising.
He longs to be a clown –
Runs about the circus top
Then somersaults to town.

Corporate Bear.

A Teddy Bear that's rather fat
Has trouble trying on his spats,
And if he's larger still than that,
Has difficulty with his hat.
To tie a cravat
Is impossible too.
(He certainly cannot buckle his shoe.)
To comb his hair is a major decision
And sadly, sometimes a cause of derision.

A Teddy Bear that's much too fat
Would rather be a lithe young chap.

Horace Bear.

Uncle Horace is a bear
Who swings a golfing club –
Likes to be a sporting bear
And joined the local club.
On every night and Thursdays
He met a golfing pro',
And practised and practised
Until allowed a go –
And at the moment he took a swing,
He whistled then for me,
Asked me to potter over
And join him at the tee.

I brought the milk and sugar
And water in a pot,
And when I'd toddled over
I realised what a clot!
I did not know the word for tea
Was spelt with just one e –

Poor Horace was embarrassed
By foolish, silly me!

Boating Bear.

When first I knew young Higgy
He knew not boats at all,
But deep within his yearning soul
He heard the ocean's call.
He longed to pull the mainsail,
To watch the curving sail,
To tack and bale and wrestle
And stand before the main.
He started with a catamaran
(Had trouble with the bung),
Moved on to dinghy racers
And then racing was begun!
Up and down the Solent
In wind and restless tides,
In racing kit and shiny oils
With buoys on every side.

On Yeoman One and Yeoman Two
And Yeoman number Three,
He spinnakered in
And spinnakered out,
And Philip came to tea,
Brought Constantine and Michael,
And the people came to see –
Oh, Higgy navigated nicely;
It cost them one and three.

They tussled with the topsail,
The mainsail and the jib –
Flicked the sheet right over
And tweeked at half a peak,
But suddenly it was alarming,
For they noticed quite a leak!
They battened down the hatches –
The bilges were so sweet –
(The deck, the stern and afters
Had been looking such a treat!)
The water came from windward
(They'd rather it was port),

And soon the wind was raging –
It was a storm – and they were caught!
The boat was tossed from left to right,
The rice was in a mess,
They had to use the elastic-band
To guide the rudder west.
The pickled eggs looked ghastly,
As did the bosun's vest,
And the compass it went crazy,
Poor Higgy did his best –
But navigating's not easy
When feeling past your best.

Well, suddenly there was a lull,
The men they gave a cheer
And peering through the telescope
The cause of strife was clear;
For port and aft
And all around
Were lots of basking whales,
Blowing through their waterspouts
And swishing with their tails.
They rolled their eyes mischievously
And gave a wicked grin,
Opened up their cavernous mouths
And then began to sing . . .
"Oh, come with us upon the sea
And have a jolly good blow,
Toss the fellows up and down
And watch the spinnakers go."

Now if you're in stormy waters
And your head is in a spin,
Think of all the sailors
And the trouble they are in.
And when you're on the ferry
And heading home to port,
Remember all the thrills and spills,
The fun of water sports!

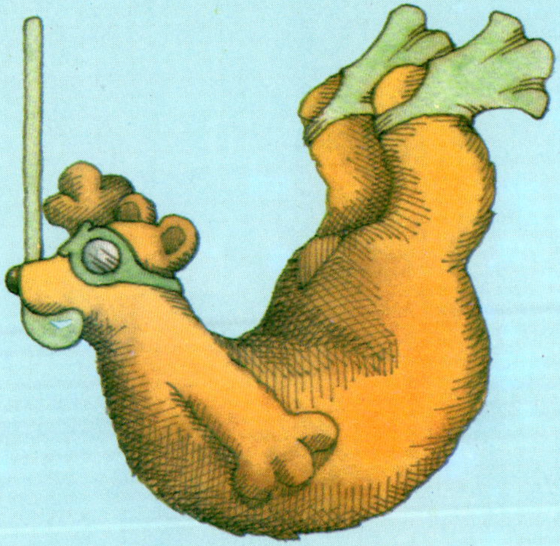

Jobbie Bear.

Jobbie is a diver.
He wears an aqualung –
Splashes in the ocean
And dives for further fun.
Smiles at all the fishes
And sees an octopus,
Stares at Lucy Catfish
And rudely calls her Puss!
Weaves the strands of seaweed
Into a floating raft,
Returns to H.M.S. Bloater
And scrambles aboard at aft.

Jobbie is a diver,
He wears an aqualung –
Splashes in the ocean
And loves his diving fun.

TITLE: **SPORTING BEARS AND OTHERS.**
Author: **Delma.**
I.S.B.N. Number: 0 948909 06 4.
PUBLISHER: DELMA DESIGN COLLECTIONS:
P.O. Box 99, 17 West Street, Alresford, Hampshire SO24 9AA, England.

SPORTING BEARS AND OTHERS. First Edition published September 10th, 1987.

I thank the talented Gwyn Wahlmann for the illustrations throughout the book.
Typesetting by my friend Roy, Typewise, Winchester.
Printed by my friends Chris Wolford, Charles and Dom, Eon Graphics, Highcliffe, Nr. Christchurch.